Rutted Field of the Heart

ALSO BY PRISCILLA WEAR ELLSWORTH

Fire Inside the Fur

When Enormous Questions Rock the World

Rutted Field of the Heart

Poems by

Priscilla Wear Ellsworth

*For Barbara Dedman
with best wishes
Priscilla Ellsworth*

Antrim House
Simsbury, Connecticut

Copyright © 2016 by Priscilla Wear Ellsworth

Except for short selections reprinted for purposes of
book review, all reproduction rights are reserved.
Requests for permission to replicate should
be addressed to the publisher.

Library of Congress Control Number: 2016931069

ISBN: 978-1-943826-03-2

First Edition, 2016

Printed & bound by United Graphics, LLC

Book design by Rennie McQuilkin

Front cover painting (detail) by Susan Rand

Photographic reproduction by Joseph Pecoraro,
Joseph's Photography, Inc., Chester, CT

Author photograph by Julia Gaviria

Antrim House
860.217.0023
AntrimHouse@comcast.net
www.AntrimHouseBooks.com
21 Goodrich Road, Simsbury, CT 06070

To Whitney

Acknowledgments

Thanks to a small family of poets: Victoria Hallerman, Wendy Larsen, Sabra Loomis, and Myra Shapiro for their close listening and response to these poems in their early stages, and to Mary Jane Nealon for helping in the selection of poems for this book. Thanks also to Rennie McQuilkin for his editorial assistance, his publishing expertise, and his generous spirit. Finally, my thanks to Susan Rand for allowing the reproduction of her painting "Cold Day" on the front cover of this volume.

I am grateful to our children, Barry, Josh, Nina, and Liza for their continuing love and laughter, and for helping me to keep alive the memory of their father. Thanks also to other family members and friends who are an essential part of my life.

Last and most deeply, I thank my husband, Whitney, with whom I shared 44 years.

Table of Contents

The Long Marriage / 3
April Fools / 4
When Peonies Bloom / 5
Love Poem, Winter / 6
After the Diagnosis / 7
Prognosis / 8
Loosestrife / 9
To Leo Beñat Ellsworth 24 Hours Old / 10
No Turning Back / 11
La Bamba / 12
In Mexico Our Grandson Dances / 13
Days of Grace / 14
Door / 15
Vermont Graveyard / 16
Looking at Bubbles on a Stream / 17
The Magician's Assistant / 18
Endless Blizzard / 20
The Wonder of Snow / 21
Deer in Winter / 22
Delft Cow / 23
We Sit Together at Dusk / 24
His Crew / 25
His Breath / 26
Last Time / 29
Dawn Fire / 30
Morning Tea / 31
New Widow / 33
The Knock / 34
Pond in Winter / 35
Spring / 36
Apple Tree / 38
Twin Seeds / 39

Frogs and Minnows / 40
Letting Down / 41
Between Worlds / 42
My Ring / 43
His Ashes / 45
Stillness at the End of Day / 46
The Visit / 47
Morning Swim / 48
The Ladder / 49
What We Loved Most About You / 51
The Gift / 52
There Was No After / 53
Through a Window / 54

ABOUT THE AUTHOR / 57

ABOUT THE BOOK / 58

*I'll love you dear, I'll love you
Till China and Africa meet,
and the river jumps over the mountain
and salmon sing in the street.*

*I'll love you till the ocean
is folded up to dry,
and the seven stars go squawking
like geese about the sky...*

from "As I Walked Out One
Evening," W.H. Auden

Rutted Field of the Heart

THE LONG MARRIAGE

You and I, how did we
get to this place, precariously perched
half way up, or is it
half way down?

As if the force that pushed us here
had receded, leaving us to sit
like a pair of boulders,
not touching or talking.

A penny for your thoughts.
You look uneasy as if you were expecting
a call from your doctor,
or something to happen with our dog.

Though the slippage of our bodies
will eventually occur,
today it is March,
the sap in the maples is rising.

Look.
Can you feel this – in the silence,
something between us is growing
rich and buttery as grass.

APRIL FOOLS

Ice fangs loosen and drip,
gutters drool like dogs
who smell their kibble.
Such is the appetite for spring
my husband and I race outside,
push our hands into dirt.
We dig, turn the soil,
chat like noisy brooks
until warm and sticky
we strip off
jackets sweaters.
Suddenly it's here again,
bare-breasted and strutting
our garden, desire
amazing us – like an ordinary robin
having tickled forth from the earth
the fatest worm.

WHEN PEONIES BLOOM

"It's like first love," he shouts,
racing an armful of soft pink blossoms
into the house.

As if a summer of first kisses
was spilling from these petals,
and he, eighteen again, giddy
with the smell of perfume.

He has fertilized the soil,
hooped the stems.
In the mud room he whistles and hums
as he arranges bunch after bunch
into bouquets.

"Come look," he says,
placing a full vase for me
on the kitchen table:
blush pink moonstones.

This time next year
these hardy plants will
unfurl their ruffled skirts,

dance triumphantly
into our house;
His voice, his whole being

alive and sensual
as the blossoms themselves
reaches out and out.

LOVE POEM, WINTER

Sometimes I think he'd be content
to burrow under with frogs and turtles,
to sleep out winter.

Nights when he nods off
with a glass or two of bourbon,
I grow uneasy.

Husband, wake up!

I promise not to hurl my words,
stir up muddy quarrels
the way I used to.

Look at our two old labs
curled up on their mat,
one licking the ear of the other.

Sweet husband, wake up!
Before the white door closes,
let's kiss and snug.

AFTER THE DIAGNOSIS

This much is sure:
you are here,
waking beside me,
dressing quietly in your slippers and robe,
as the falling snow is dressing
the trees and bushes.

You are here, and gone
from our room now,
as you are every morning,
making coffee in the kitchen,
letting the dogs out for their morning run.

In a few months trees will bud,
birds will sing at our window,
another season will come.
Like the snow on the branches
you might not be here.

But this much is sure:
you are here now,
your hands bringing me enormous joy
in a small mug of green tea.

PROGNOSIS

We thought we were prepared,
but the doctor's words
"three to six months"

knocked us flat;
my husband's face blanched white,
I could hardly breathe.

He sat on the metal table,
I on the chair,

as if an unexpected wave had smacked us,
filling our eyes and mouth
with sand.

No, no, you can't get through this. . .

But we do. Like so many others
who'd walked through this door,
we reach for each other's hands.

We stumble to our feet, find air,
go on.

LOOSESTRIFE

While they are still in blossom, our son uproots
ten stalks of purple loosestrife,
packs them in plastic bags and burns them.
He doesn't want these invasive weeds
to take over the pond bank, displace
the cattails and jewelweed.

Loosestrife. The disconsolate name pulls me
to the day our six-year-old daughter was Hope
in a school play. The last to make her way out
of Pandora's box, she flew around the classroom.
With her golden hair and tutu,
she chased away countless black-clad sorrows.

Fallujah, Mozambique, Bagdad –
strife is on the loose,
discord and chaos sinking
roots into villages, mountains,
deserts, seashores.

And closer to home, disease has invaded
my husband's body, has spread
from pancreas, to liver, to spleen.
He has weeks, months, if he's lucky.

Hope, crouching inside the dark
of a box, push open the lid.

TO LEO BEÑAT ELLSWORTH
24 HOURS OLD

Wake up, sleepy boy.

On this fine November day,
the sun trumpets your arrival.

On the Charles a flottila of mergansers
gathers to salute you;
geese fly past the window barking
good luck, good omens.

Wake up, sleepy boy.

While you sleep in your heated lair,
your father and grandfather talk loudly of war
as if you were not here.

Leo, wake up and have some milk;
the world your mother's breast is
waits to feed you.

NO TURNING BACK

This winter he packs in trips to Vermont,
San Francisco, Mexico,

takes trail rides with grandchildren
though the Sierra Madre mountains.

At home, wanting to leave things in order,
he cleans out books, papers.

Today carrying a box from the barn,
he notices a robin flying over the snow.

An eagerness for spring
in his steps, he rushes with the news.

Tucked in the cold angle
between wing and abyss is the hope

he will maintain his stride
long enough to celebrate his May
birthday, see
his favorite tree peonies in bloom.

LA BAMBA

Sitting on a shoe shine stand
in San Miguel de Allende,
my husband in a straw hat
gets his old leather shoes shined,
while in a corner of the jardin, near him,
out grandchildren dance
to mariachi music.

My husband, who loves parties,
ties a napkin around his forhead and dances
with abandon at family weddings,
has a few months to live.

The shoe man rubs and polishes.
The four street musicians
in their silver-studded charros
blast out *La Bamba*.

Arriba! Arriba!

My husband's eyes fill with laughter and tears
as the children shake and shimmie,
dance wildly, stomping their feet
with joy.

IN MEXICO
OUR GRANDSON DANCES

and chants *baila baila baila*,
moving his whole body to the music
of Julieta Venega, or a wind-up spider toy.
As if rhythm and body were one
windy tree, he holds his arms out, sways
this way, that way
like the jacaranda outside the window.
Rhythm and music at the root
of who he is, *mi nieto*
is teaching me a new language;
soft-beated sounds fall
from his mouth like purple petals.
I sweep them up, carry them with me:
arana, abuela, bailabailabaila.

DAYS OF GRACE

His sudden illness whirled in on us
like a white storm, wiping away
the small hurts in our long marriage.

I stopped nagging him about his weight,
he no longer chided me
about my being a health nut.

As if love's knuckled fist had slipped
into a white glove, for five months
hardly a cross word passed between us.

What if we had lived like this all our days?
If we had known long ago
the exact night he would die,

would it have changed
how we planned our trips, spoke to each other,
made cups of tea, made love?

DOOR

All summer the door was swollen shut.
No matter how hard I pried and pulled
it would not open.

Birdsongs were muffled, the scent
of peonies blocked,
nests of bobolinks went unnoticed.

Now that the air is dryer, cooler,
the wooden frame has come unstuck,
the door opens.

The maple that shades our house
lets loose its leaves, flocks of starlings
take off for someplace else.

Our house echoes with the sound
of honking geese, the smell
of humus and rotting apples.

Now that death has a foot in the door,
I couldn't shut it tight
if I wanted to.

VERMONT GRAVEYARD

Wind rushes over the orange hills,
sweeping maple leaves against the stones.
Weeds brush against the markers.

My husband and I kneel down,
read the inscriptions:

Behold as you pass by
as you are living so once was I.

Here lies my friend
till time shall end.

He walks me to the spot
where his mother and father sleep.
Next to it an empty plot
covered by a patch of wild thyme.

That night we lie in bed,
not touching or talking,
as if we had invisible boxes around us.

LOOKING AT BUBBLES ON A STREAM

His mouth like a fire box
from chemo,
bouts of diarrhea, loss of hair.

My husband put himself through this agony
to extend life by a few months.

Why does he do this?
For family? To bring to completion
a project on the South Sudan?
To see the peonies he planted
once again come into bloom?

Lighter than water, molecules of air
bead up into bubbles,
move along the surface of the stream.

Bubbles don't witness the bluebells on the bank,
or notice the kingfisher's rapid wing beat.

They don't fight
the current, or worry
how long they'll exist.

Unlike us, and like us
they simply go on
until they don't.

THE MAGICIAN'S ASSISTANT

All he had to do was whisper
the word *light*
and the throats of birds

opened, the pale pink
of dawn deepened
into the red of fox fur.

Some mornings he lugged sac-like clouds
over our fields, dropped gifts
of rain to make roses bloom,

or slipped from his damp pockets
a yellow iris, or a black
scarf of water.

Often he would unwind from his ear
the howl of a dog, or make a mountain
vanish.

Who else could take separate days
of the year and knot them
into one long string.

Who else could link
and unlink our lives
like silver rings.

I feared getting close.

Still, nights when he donned
a black silk jacket and pulled
stars out of his sleeves,

a part of me yearned to be his assistant,
to be the moon he could sever
and make whole again.

ENDLESS BLIZZARD

My husband, head down
over a clipboard,
thumbs through layers
of papers and forms.

He groans, puts down facts
as if he were dropping
one foot in front of the other.

Little by little the world
of medicine is annihilating him.

This winter trudging from appointment
to appointment is like a dream
neither of us can wake from:
as if he were pushing his way down
one long corridor of snow
after another.

As if he were walking deeper
into a whitened room.

THE WONDER OF SNOW

He mumbled he was too tired
to get out of bed.
I couldn't accept what the cancer was doing;
black-fisted thoughts
pummeled my head.

I pulled a second blanket over him,
dressed and went outside.

A light snow was falling,
covering all the places where we'd walked,
the lawn, the fields behind the barn,
the path around the pond.

Without effort the snow was falling,
slipping a fresh white coat
on the scrawny box bush,
the leafless trees.

As I stood there,
the wall around our garden softened;
flakes brushed against my eyelids,
a few fell onto my tongue.

Slowly, I could feel the quiet of snow
melting into my body.

There is a Zen saying:
No snowflake ever falls in the wrong place.

My husband was safe in his bed
when I went back to him.

DEER IN WINTER

This winter a bitter cold drives them
deeper into our lives.
In the middle of the day they paw
the field in back of our barn,
or come to our garden to browse
a curled-up rhododendron.

Today we catch a young doe in the act
of nibbling a *Cornus alba* we carefully planted
to mark our boundary.

When we wave our hands in the air
to scare her off, she casually lifts her head,
turns towards us as if to say
I, too, have a right.

Standing stock still she watches us
burlap the box bush;
her dark eyes eat into us, with a look
as deep and beautiful as this land.

DELFT COW

Asked to repair our delft cow,
glue back the horn and tit
our cat had chewed,

Mr. Fixit said, yes, he could,
come back in a couple of weeks.

His hands shook like the stairs
we had walked up to find him.
Still, we left our cow on the counter.

Six months, a year, two went by.
The store on Madison Avenue was closed.
The rumor was Mr. Fixit took to drink,
couldn't fix himself.

The delft cow was part of my husband's childhood,
broken, mended, broken again –
each crack held part of him.
He loved it. I loved it.
It belonged in the center of our Vermont table.

We wanted it back, the peaceful pasture scene,
the milkmaid on her stool, milking.

Instead, we walk busy Manhattan streets,
bellowing to ourselves like weaned calves.
Tit or no tit, Mr. Fixit,
return our cow.

WE SIT TOGETHER AT DUSK

On the porch watching
the colors of the sky fade
from bright blue to pale blue
to white.

Without sound or effort
the day simply dissolves around us,
like a fabric worn out
from sunlight or over-washing.

The dark coming on,
I move closer; he takes my hand,
squeezes it tight.

HIS CREW

He gathers his stricken family
around him, gives each of us tasks.

"You can take care of me," he says.
I run to the drug store for medicines.
One sister takes on hospice, a daughter the memorial.

Like a ship's crew, our family,
handling the sails and ropes.

The thing that matters most
is to keep him afloat,
to help him reach his destination safely.

His legs swell with fluid,
sores apear in his mouth.
Still, he is clear, decisive.

As he gets weaker, he talks openly
about death.

"It's going fast, fast," he whispers
that last day.

Our son reads him a book about fishing,
another gives him drops of morphine,
I rub his feet with cream.
Love doing all that it can…

HIS BREATH

After the morphine,
his body falls into a deep calm.

No more mucous rattle,
no more heaving up from the bed.

What had been a fierce raking
tide now laps, lulls
him to sleep.

I sit by his side listening
as each breath pulls back like a wave
to gather strength
for the next.

I count out the seconds,
note the pauses between breaths getting longer
and longer.

Can he hear the sea quieting down inside him,
feel the stroking of hands on his forehead,
"I love you, love you"
whispered in his ear.

*

All afternoon he doesn't move;
only his chest moves.
We sit around the room breathing with him,
his sons and daughters, two sisters;
grandchildren tiptoe in and out.

"It's boring in here," a five-year-old sighs,
"Pa looks half dead."

An alert stillness
hunches over my husband.
Peering below the flattened surface
of his breath, it waits
for a darting shadow,
a shift of wind, a sign.

*

It is past midnight.
Songs from the Auvergne
play softly in the background.

A lapping sound lulls me.

Comforted by the ongoing swoosh of sea,
I am dozing with my eldest daughter
on the queen bed
when my other daughter,
breathing with him,
wakes me.

I sit upright.
The silence washing over the room
tells me
there is no next.

*

Through a fog of sobs
and farewell kisses
I can almost make out
rising from the stilled body
a swelling spinnaker of light
sailing him who-is-no-longer-him
out past rocks, boats, stars.

*

No more swells in his chest
heaving up and down.

No more sound of his gravelly breath,
of the tide raking back and forth
over rocks.

But listen.

Somewhere, right now
the sea is singing…

What was my husband's breath
is entering the lungs
of a newborn.

LAST TIME

I have spent the night with his body.
I have blessed it with kisses, and given thanks.

Outside a white van pulls up,
a man opens the back doors,
pulls out a gurney.

So this is it.

I run my fingers over his cold cheeks,
his forehead, his nose, his ears.

I praise his body with my tears.

The coroner tells me it is best
if I step out of the room.

My hands and lips, warm with life,
touch him for the last time.

Good-bye dear man I have loved,
who showed me how to live,
and how to die.

Good-bye to your fine tight curls,
your brow wrinkled with thought.

Good-bye to your cornflower blue eyes,
your big and patient heart,
your smile, your long aristocratic feet.

DAWN FIRE

Before dawn the hunters are up
and in their blinds.

First light brings the sound of guns
and the red trumpeting of geese
as the flock takes flight.

I rush to the window, see
a long dark thread pulling its way
over the cornstubble.

Where the thread unspools from,
swamp or dream, is uncertain.
But like the breath of the living, it never fails

one end reaches into the new day
while the other

knots on my ribs
tighter and tighter
each time a bird is shot down.

MORNING TEA

Rising from a dream, sorrow
shuffles to the kitchen, wearing
my husband's plum colored robe.

Half awake we talk with an intimacy
as if we had known each other
a long time.

I report who called in the night,
complain about the sink not working.

When I get up to put on a kettle,
sorrow watches, advising me
to go slowly – it's important,

sorrow says, not to rush,
to take all the time you need,
to feel what you feel.

I pull down a bone-white tea pot
from the shelf.

I rub its neck,
its foot,
its round hard belly.

I hold it gently in my hands
the way my hands held
my husband's face that last morning.

Slowly I fill the tea pot,
put on the cover.

Like green tea leaves,
I steep in loss.

NEW WIDOW

Questions are trowels
that unearth nothing.

Words . . .
put them away.

I am not ready, not ready.

Grief needs a long winter
in which to rest.

For now my heart is a garden
that cannot be turned.

THE KNOCK

Let me in, let me in,
if only for a few hours.

I have news from your brothers and sisters,
a bearskin

to warm you, a knapsack filled with raisins
and honey, pine twigs for the fire.

If you wish I could put up a pot
of your favorite Hu-kwa tea.

Can you hear me rapping,
shaking the window?

When you held my face in your hands for the last time,
your tears and kisses were like water to me.

Darling, don't send me away tonight.
The road through the deep snow was long.

POND IN WINTER

Ice erases nothing:
not the blood-sucking leaches
or croaking frogs.

They're all down there, beneath
the glazed surface.

Why fret like the wild goose
beating its chest and wings against
ice to keep winter doors open?

Desires pass through seasons.
Accept what is
for now. Banked under,

the fire in us,
like the olive salamanders,
asleep on the bottom.

SPRING

The first warm April day
the earth softens, begins to open.

Flowerbeds barren all winter
suddenly pulse with color.
Yellow wood poppies
stick their heads out of dirt
and fat stalks of blood root.

I kneel in the garden,
half-heartedly turning the soil,
careful not to disturb
new shoots of bleeding heart.

Robins looking for worms
resume their annual
stop-start dance on the lawn.

Two squirrels chasing each other
around a tree, leap
from branch to branch.

A cardinal whistles
what-cheer-cheer-cheer
what-cheer-cheer-cheer.

My husband belongs here…I see him
eagerly wheeling cartloads of mulch,
baggy jeans, straw hat on his head…

I hoop the peonies, stake the lilies,
do tasks he used to do, the reality
of his absence digging deeper
and deeper in.

I put down my tools.

APPLE TREE

The collapse was inaudable.
It wasn't until morning that I knew
our favorite apple tree had rotted,
split apart.

One half still stood,
but the flowering branches facing our bedroom
were missing.

All summer I checked on the tree.
Its shape was thinner,
more angular, but it continued
to put out green

I wrote thank you notes, shopped, cooked,
did much of what I had done before.

Last evening, after three days of rain,
what was left of the tree
fell, as if it couldn't hold the weight
of its loss.

TWIN SEEDS

One arrived one evening
when I was listening
to the songs from the Auvergne,
a recording we often played,
the other unexpectedly when I picked up
a red pepper in the market.

His death had turned me
to fertile ground.
Still, I thought, *they're temporary visitors –
having hitched rides
on notes of music, hairs of light,
they won't stay long.*

I never believed
those twin seeds would settle
in the rutted field of my heart,
with time split
their husks, unpack
roots and branches.

FROGS AND MINNOWS

for Pablo

Pant legs rolled up, I stand in a brook
with a five-year-old boy,
both of us clutching nets.

He bends down to scoop up a minnow
but misses. Over and over
he scoops and misses.

It's a beautiful August day,
a few leaves in the surrounding woods
beginning to turn.

The determined boy tries and tries.
This time it's a frog he's after.
I look down at an eddy swirling

at my feet, two opposing currents
holding me in a place where I am both
young boy and aging woman

eager to catch something, and happy
if my net is filled with nothing.

LETTING DOWN

All weekend my spirits were held aloft
by grandchildren. Stretched full

and happy I flew here, there
like a taut balloon tied to their fists,

a string of arguments, laughter
pulling me from room to room.

As if joy were nothing but a brief
bagful of air,

now that they're gone, I collapse,
face the endless task of learning

once again how to be alone.

BETWEEN WORLDS

No matter how many times
a skein of geese fly over our house
I stop what I'm doing and look up.
Whether they're in a strict
V formation, a single line
or in a state of flux,
I think of our family,
sisters, brothers, cousins,
coming together from afar
for a marriage, or funeral.
After the bride and groom cut
the cake, or the casket
is lowered into the ground
and we depart, I hear us
calling to each other,
the living to the dead,
the dead to the living –
u-whonk u-whonk
u-whonk u-whonk.

MY RING

No ordinary gold band for me.
I had to have that shimmering ring
in Van Cleef & Arpels on Fifth, the ring
with the enameled blue dome,
sparkling with diamond lights.

I wasn't going to be marked,
grounded like other women.
This was the sixties, and I wanted

a ring that would float me
to the Mediterranean night sky,
and the Blue Mosque in Istanbul.

So my husband-to-be bought it,
slipped it on my finger,
the ring blessed by the minister.

This ring, sometimes forgotten
on a sill or a bureau,
has always returned

to summon the words
we spoke long ago
in a small church by the sea.

Dearest beloved, now that we have kept
our vows, through joy and sickness,
and death has come,

does us part,
more than ever I cherish
this globed ring.

I wear it on my finger
to hold you close.

This starry dome, the token of freedom
under which we sailed,
has become my anchor.

HIS ASHES

To the bobolinks nesting in the hayfield,
to the monarchs feeding on milkweed,

to the timothy and clover,
the sedge grass and pond water,

I give these ashes.

To the bittern hiding in the cattails,
the beaver asleep in his lodge,

to the light, cloud, hawk,
moving through air,

I give these ashes.

To our sons, daughters, grandchildren
who will inherit this farm,

to those who have died
and those yet to be born,

I open my hand, release these ashes.

STILLNESS AT THE END OF DAY

There's a stillness at the end of day,
as if the argument

between wind and grasses
has been settled.

Trees stand motionless.
Doves cease.

No farmer whistling home his dog,
no hawk diving.

It's as if the world were pausing
to take a deep breath,

to listen to whatever is rising
within and without us.

THE VISIT

He slips in with the light
between my sleep and waking,

tiptoes around the room
as if looking for something,
a pair of glasses, a walking stick.

Coming close to my bed, he leans
his face close to mine,
as if to tell me something.

Is it a kiss he wants? Or a book on Emerson
hidden under the pillow?
Like the light he moves in silence.

The moment he died, I was dozing.

His dying woke me, I rushed to his side.
I kissed his lips, rubbed his feet.

This morning
my husband comes like a whisper, and leaves
no footprint on the rug.

MORNING SWIM

A cool summer morning, a low
vaporous cloud hovering
over our pond.

I stand on the bank looking for you
taking your daily swim,
our black lab paddling fast behind.

Today no dog splashes,
no man naked but for a straw hat
breast-strokes his way to the other side.

You are not here, and yet

your absence is itself a presence.

I call out your name,
throw off my towel, jump in.

THE LADDER

The children and I won't dizzy
when we see a ladder
rising out of the barn,
unfolding into blue,

won't rush out and scream
about thorns, bones,
the tumbling sky.

God willing,
my husband will climb
to the highest rung.

He'll plaster our dark
with snow, twist
the moon globe
tight in its socket.

As he stakes up clouds,
his frown will hang
like a warning

over ungrouted cracks
in the silo, holes
in the cow shed.

Any place we live can survive
as a body cannot.
My husband knows this.

When he climbs back down
we'll dress him
in an old grey workshirt,
slick with sweat and grease,
baggy jeans gone at the knees,

place in his hands
hammer, screwdriver, wrench,
tools he'll need to shore up
roofs and gutters.

WHAT WE LOVED MOST ABOUT YOU

You are done now
with shooting pheasants,
casting flies for rainbows,
done with telling family stories,
with reading Yeats,
Sakharov, Dostoevsky.

You are through now
with hooping peonies, with planting
wood poppies and double blood root.

Others will take up the fight
for prisoners of conscience,
will cook the Thanksgiving turkey.

Someone more skilled at carpentry
will repair our broken table.

Younger men will race out
to be first on the dance floor.
But none will tie a checkered napkin
around his forehead,
hold a carnation between his teeth.

No, they won't be you, my love,
lit up with wedding music and champagne,
stomping your long aristocratic feet,
lighting a fire in the toes
of every woman in the room.

THE GIFT

Two seasons have passed
since you've been gone.

Still I rush to you to complain
the sink is clogged,

share with you the good news
of our son's job.

Why should death come between us?

This evening walking the hayfield
you and I often circled

your clipped, gravelly voice emerges
from a chorus of crickets and frogs.

I have heard your voice many times,
but this evening it is a gift

I unwrap slowly.

THERE WAS NO AFTER

It was all here,
in the snow falling on the street,
in the shiny redness of a pepper.

It was in his hands fixing
a leaking sink, in his knees
kneeling in dirt staking the monkshood;

in training and running his dogs,
cooking pancakes at family breakfasts,
reciting Yeats and Auden.

It was in the work to be done
for prisoners of conscience,
the words and deeds.

Wading into a stream in hip boots,
casting for a rainbow or brook trout
was as close to heaven as he desired.

If a higher being existed, it resided
in the tree peonies that opened
in his garden each May.

My husband lives on

in a stack of Sunday morning cakes,
the green thumbs of our son,
a sparrow pecking at seeds in a dung heap.

THROUGH A WINDOW

I watched as the coroner wheeled your body away.
With my own hands I scattered your ashes.

And yet this morning in the kitchen,
peeling the skin off a peach,
I saw you through a window.

You were in the garden,
tamping in plugs of rosemary and thyme.

I called your name, *Whitney,* and you turned,
started to walk towards . . .

Just then a neighbor's dog barked,
you disappeared.

I don't know who dressed you
in your baggy jeans,
led you into the garden.

I do know you exist.
I saw you through a window.

ABOUT THE AUTHOR

Priscilla Wear Ellsworth grew up on a farm outside Philadelphia. After receiving an M.A. in art history from Columbia University, she married, raised two children, and taught poetry workshops in New York City public schools. A grandmother of six, she spends many happy hours with family and a fifteen-year-old dog. She is a long-time member of Amnesty International, working for the release of prisoners of conscience around the world. *Rutted Field of the Heart* is her third poetry collection. Her poems have twice been nominated for a Pushcart Prize and have appeared in various journals including *Cape Rock, Connecticut River Review, Whetstone, and Nimrod.* She currently lives in Salisbury, Connecticut.

This book is set in Garamond Premier Pro, which had its genesis in 1988 when type-designer Robert Slimbach visited the Plantin-Moretus Museum in Antwerp, Belgium, to study its collection of Claude Garamond's metal punches and typefaces. During the mid-fifteen hundreds, Garamond—a Parisian punch-cutter—produced a refined array of book types that combined an unprecedented degree of balance and elegance, for centuries standing as the pinnacle of beauty and practicality in type-founding. Slimbach has created an entirely new interpretation based on Garamond's designs and on compatible italics cut by Robert Granjon, Garamond's contemporary.

To order additional copies of this book
or other Antrim House titles, contact the publisher at

Antrim House
21 Goodrich Rd., Simsbury, CT 06070
860.217.0023, AntrimHouse@comcast.net
or the house website (www.AntrimHouseBooks.com).

•

On the house website
in addition to information on books
you will find sample poems, upcoming events,
and a "seminar room" featuring supplemental biography,
notes, images, poems, reviews, and
writing suggestions.